# Octaviaisms Confusion Says

## Octavia McKinney

Text Copyright © 2018 by Octavia McKinney

Illustrations Copyright © 2018 by Jesy Arriaga

All rights reserved. This book or any portion thereof may not be reproduced or used in any manner whatsoever without the express written permission of the publisher except for the use of brief quotations in a book review.

ISBN 978-1-947635-00-5 (Hardback Edition)
ISBN 978-1-947635-02-9 (Paperback Edition)
ISBN 978-1-947635-03-6 (Coloring Book Edition)

Printed in the United States of America

First Printing January 2018

Published by Octavia Ink

Imagine yourself
with nothing…no
sight, smell, hearing,
taste and touch.
Now picture yourself.
You're blessed,
aren't you?

**The Faults you see lie deep within yourself, not another person.**

The truth
is real,
but can
you be
real about
the truth.

Did you remind yourself to breathe today?
**I mean really breathe.**

*Feet give you balance. Buy shoes. It's protection for your balance. Like a bandage.*

*A life unloved is only when you haven't found yourself.*

When you listen to the words people tell you, tell me they make sense, when every voice sounds different, yet they are the same language. Apparently.

How real do you feel when you know you are actually made up of 57%-60% water?

**Equality is
the balance
of life.
We are
all bad
and good.**

*Sacrifice is best done not to another but for another.*

*Where do you think you stand? Try not to stand, but to float. No hard landing.*

*So, for anyone who thinks they're better than another, do you bleed differently?*

*If you think you're sane, think about the way you dance. Break it down and realize none of it makes sense. Even if you're trained. You're in the craziest of motion.*

*Standing above others* only means you don't understand sitting and relaxing with them.

If you truly want to feel, stop moving and watch, move slowly and watch again. Then compare. Are you an octopus, an ostrich, an armadillo, or just you, or just life?

We all tell tales, but the tallest tales we can come up with are those that we have endured. The worst and the best all come from your reality. Write fun stuff and it will come back tenfold.

It's hard to believe
that we are worthy.
Yet who's taking
the tally but ourselves?

So erase the chalkboard
and give yourself
some points.

                    Maybe a lot more.

*I'd like to see the whole world dance now. Forget all the bad stuff and just dance. When everything means nothing, but the body just moves like the music. It takes away that bad feeling.*

What's your favorite smell or sound? Now hold onto it and breathe. Now live as if you're always surrounded by it.

Move like you love the clothes, and the world will love them, too.

How much time does it take to hug a person? Now think how much time it took to not hold them.
You're wasting time.

*Think of the population and the possibility of what you could do to make that population better. It relies on all of us, but it starts with you.*

Have you ever realized that there is a pet that doesn't understand the language you speak because he's not from the same country?

What have you done without? What if you had one thing and gave it to one person and they did the same? Wow. We would all have something.

Forever is an imaginary thing because you won't be here to see it. But imagine seeing one great thing happen. Now do it. **Together we can create forever.**

How will you hold yourself up to everything you have done? The same way you hold your friends up, with gentleness.

If ever you feel like nothing, don't worry. Because if you put all those nothings together, they add up to something.

Having one true
friend is better
than a room full of
unreliable ones.

Learn to love.
For everything
is better
when studied
and practiced.

I will teach you to fly,
but I ask you not to clip
my wings because we can
soar together.

Sad news can bring sadness. Yet sadness can elevate happiness because of the opposition.

*Enjoy life, it's the best revenge.*

Try as you might to think that someone is better than you, but apparently you were enough to compare to them. So within this equation, you're enough.

How does one question oneself when they put themselves into the equation?

*Once again you are relevant.*

Forgiveness is freedom.

Trying to destroy the ones you hate, only means that they were a challenge to you. You're so cool...I mean envious.

If ever someone says you haven't done anything, say, at least I haven't done anything wrong, like insulting someone, but I can do something right.

There are an infinite amount of opportunities. They are like stars in the sky. Just pick one, focus on it, and you will see the light.

As bleak as things seem, I can say the sun comes up and the moon is there for you to dance with, even when no one is looking.

**The tears you have
are the feelings
that some wish
they have.
Some are at a loss
without feeling.**

Why haven't you started doing what you want? Don't worry. Just think about it as the end of you stopping what you haven't done, and the beginning of what you will do.

*Settle down* can mean spending the rest of your life with someone or stop doing that.

The calm before the storm is safe. Enjoy the storm, it's more exciting.

*To say the least sometimes says the most.*

Sound out your words
before you speak.

Now you have a chance
to be efficient.

There's an empty seat on a crowded train; stand and think of how lucky you are that you're not deserted.

Sound advice is only useful
if you're listening.

*Being into bondage is ironic, because it's actually freedom for those who adore it.*

Imagine yourself naked and judge. Now imagine yourself as a baby imagining yourself naked. Now try to judge yourself as that baby. You can't, huh?

**If you have nothing now, you have the possibility of anything.**

Count to ten, now count to ten backwards. Now count on yourself because you learned how to count.

Spend time with those who mean something to you and mean something to those who spend time with you.

*Resistance of your fate
is real living.*

*Practicality is most useful in impractical situations.*

*Know to leave
all situations
if you don't
gain knowledge
from them.
You just learned
something,
so leave and
move forward.*

*Resolution comes after a revolution of questioning.*

*Faults usually exist because someone faltered.*

Enter every day with joy and leave life knowing you gave joy.

The only finality you should **ever** experience is finding your **true love**.

Passion has many meanings.
Mean to have passion for
many things.

*If someone says anything negative, I just pretend I don't speak their language. It's kinda true. I don't understand negativity.*

I PROMISE TO TEACH YOU TO FLY, EVEN IF YOU FLY AWAY.

How much time have you wasted?
It's not possible to get it back
but there are infinite ways you
can make up for it.

SETTLING IS
A WASTE OF
TIME,
TRY SETTING
UP FOR A
GOOD TIME.

*The touch of someone who loves you is more than enough.*

Losing oneself in another is ironic,
because it's not a loss at all.

Falling in love is only possible when you're willing to soar higher.

*Crying is a way you remind yourself of your humanity.*

Your biggest goal is to start, not to finish.

Creativity is the beginning of a great story.

If you really want to touch me, all you have to do is smile. I'm touched.

*Sadness is just a way of recognizing happiness.*

Salvation is acceptance.

*Set your standards high enough that no one else can knock them down.*

Denial is only a path that will eventually lead you away from the truth.

Envy is a reminder that you're not perfect, *but don't hold on to it or belittle yourself or others with it.*

The best present
is
to be present.

**Callousness is
a *choice*
and *unrewarded*.**

Fear is escapable if you open your eyes to the other possibilities.

*The unspoken word creates a broken heart. Say you love someone.*

Fascination can become dangerous if not applied correctly.

*Indifference is thinking something doesn't matter; everything is matter and matters.*

Your greatest reality is being real to yourself.

*What is your greatest regret? It should be thinking about regrets.*

*Stillness is when you notice life and its movement most.*

*A human's most obvious flaw

is trying to prove

power over another.*


*True power is

acceptance of another.*

As a matter of fact,
contrary to
popular opinion,
your opinion matters.

Standing tall is bending over backwards for others.

Your tears are filled with salt water, but so are the oceans, and think of how beautiful they are.

Popularity is a way of pretending importance. True importance is making lack of pretense popular.

***Empathy is
an essential*** strength.

Loss is a necessary evil, to remind you of what you should cherish.

**Intimacy is greatest when selfless.**

Self awareness happens only when you recognize others.

*How much time did it take for you to read this when you honestly could have spent more time on hugging a kitten or doing what you really should be doing?*

www.ingramcontent.com/pod-product-compliance
Lightning Source LLC
Chambersburg PA
CBHW041507220426
43661CB00017B/1268